The Open University

Start Writing

A practical introduction to creative writing

David Stephenson

To purchase a selection of Open University course materials visit http://www.ouw.co.uk, or for a catalogue, contact Open University Worldwide, Michael Young Building, Walton Hall, Milton Keynes MK7 6AA, United Kingdom: tel. + 44 (0)1908 858785; fax + 44 (0)1908 858787; email ouw-customer-services@open.ac.uk

Alternatively you may visit the Open University website at http://www.open.ac.uk where you can learn more about the wide range of courses and packs offered at all levels by The Open University.

The Open University

Walton Hall, Milton Keynes

MK7 6AA

First published 2007

The Open University would like to recognise the cooperation of Linda Anderson and the Arts Faculty of The Open University.

Designed and typeset by Hannah Brunt

Cartoon illustrations by Heather Clarke

Pencil and sharpener image (page 7) © Owen Price (Istockphoto.com)

Printed and bound in the United Kingdom by [printer]

ISBN 978 0 7492 2698 5

1.1

Contents

Introduction

Welcome

...to Start Writing, The Open University's introduction to creative writing.

Writing can be one of the most rewarding things you can do with your spare time. It requires no expensive equipment – a pencil stub and the back of an envelope can be enough to get you started – and it can be done anywhere, at any time. That said, writing is a skill like any other, requiring patience and perseverance, and the aim of this book is to provide you with some of the techniques needed to get you started.

Before that, however, what do we mean by creative writing? It is fair to say that a shopping list has little evidence of creativity, but almost all other forms of writing – biography and autobiography, fiction and non-fiction, poetry, plays, critical reviews, letters to family and friends, even university essays – have, to a greater or lesser extent, some element of creativity. By this, we mean that you, the writer, will have invested the work with elements that only you could have generated, using patterns of words and an inter-relation of ideas that are unique to you. It follows from this that no-one can teach you to write creatively, but what a book like this can do is open your mind to new ways of expressing yourself, and show you how to craft your work in ways that will be more satisfying to reader and writer alike.

As will become clear, the book is mainly aimed at newcomers who want to start writing fiction – chiefly short stories or novels – but budding playwrights and poets may also find something of use in the following pages, as might slightly more experienced but still unpublished writers. At the back of the book you will find details of a number of Open University courses especially dedicated to these other forms of writing, as well as courses that will enable you to learn more about writing fiction, to expand your writing horizons even further.

The Book

...consists of the following main sections

Beginnings

- Before we begin...
- Get the idea

Middles

- Developing characters
- Developing plots
- Structures

Endings

- Editing and rewriting
- Marketing your work

as well as a resource section highlighting specific topics. The section titles should not be taken to imply that all works of fiction ought to have a beginning, middle and end in the traditional sense – many short stories, for example, focus on a single illuminating event – but rather that the process of writing has three phases: generating ideas, writing them down, and honing the first draft into a finished work. Each step is essential, but the real **craft** of writing – the real creativity, if you like – lies in that all-important final phase. It's at this stage that the writer manipulates the text so that her/his ideas, so clear and fresh in the mind's eye, are translated into two dimensions – black marks on a white background – in such a way that the reader gets as close as possible to the original vision. It is not easy, but therein lies the skill of writing, its real pleasure and its reward.

But enough of introductions – let's get down to it!

Beginnings

- Before we begin...
- Get the idea

Notes

Before we begin...

Firstly, why do you want to write? People write for a number of reasons – self-expression, exploring ideas that cannot for a variety of reasons be explored in the real world, externalising thoughts that they do not have the opportunity to voice aloud, leaving something of themselves for posterity, making money – but the last of these should also be the least. The fact is that there are hundreds of thousands of writers in the UK but only a handful who make a living from their writings. Even many well-respected novelists, poets and playwrights have to augment their incomes by taking other jobs, so you would be well advised not to start with the idea that this book will set you on the road to fame and fortune. It may well do so, of course – we sincerely hope it does – but that should never be your primary intention. Instead, you should write for all those other reasons – and any others that may be personal to you – but primarily for the pleasures it can bring to you and, hopefully, to your readers.

Secondly – and this brings us to the first exercise – what do you read?

Exercise

To start, make a list of the last five or six books you read. What do they have in common? Are they fiction or non-fiction? Are they by the same author or all of the same genre? If you most recently read magazines rather than books, what sorts of magazine were they?

Expand the list by taking a close look at your bookshelves/magazine rack. What sorts of books/magazines predominate? (You should actually look at your collection rather than relying on memory – you may be surprised!)

Next, what do you want to produce? Is it your ambition to write the sort of novel that is regularly reviewed in the broadsheets, and tends to get short-listed for the Man Booker prize, or are you more tempted by what is usually referred to as genre fiction: romances, thrillers, science fiction, fantasy etc? Alternatively, do you fancy trying your hand at short stories rather than novels, or non-fiction books/articles rather than either? If you are interested in producing more than one type of work, make another list ranking them in order.

Now compare the two lists. Are they the same or remarkably different? If different, why do you think that is so?

This may seem like a strange sort of exercise for a writing course, but analysing your reading habits is a very useful first step. Your two lists may be very similar, in which case your path will be relatively straightforward, but they may throw up some anomalies that will be worth resolving before we go any further.

It is not unusual, for example, for people who mainly read biographies to want to write a 'literary' novel. Nor is it unusual for those who read detective fiction to want to write a romance. The reasons for this might be numerous – a single book that has made such a strong impression that it has overshadowed everything else you have ever read, for example – but quite often it is because the prospective writer does not believe that she/he has the specialist skills required to produce work in a certain field. But why should this be so? After all, who knows more about the conventions and patterns of a thriller than those who read them regularly? Who knows more about what a reader wants from a romance than someone who avidly devours them*? In short, nothing could be simpler – plan to write in the genre to which you are most accustomed. If you want to write a different sort of book, then start reading more!

The other point, of course, is that all writers should read as widely as possible, if only to lay themselves open to the technical and stylistic influences of a wide range of other authors. You don't want to copy slavishly the style of a particular writer, but taking on board how a number of different writers work with the language will enable your own authorial voice to emerge. It follows from this that you should start to read **as a writer**, not just for the storyline but also for the different ways in which writers achieve their effects. The best way to start doing this is to re-read a book by a favourite author, but this time looking at the way the sentences and paragraphs are structured, the way in which characters are introduced, how they handle dialogue etc.

*It is worth noting that the down-market reputation of romantic fiction is undeserved. The books may be somewhat formulaic, and not to everyone's taste, but on the whole they are well-written, professional pieces of work ...and not at all easy to write!

Exercise

Select your favourite book/story. Read twice through the opening paragraph or even the first page – the first time for pure enjoyment, the second time with a critical eye. Ask yourself the following questions:

How does the first sentence catch your attention?

How smoothly do the next few sentences follow on from the first and draw you into the story? How does the end of the first paragraph/page make you want to go on to the second paragraph/page?

Now read it for a third time, delving even more deeply. Ask yourself the following:

If it's a description – of a place (a landscape, a street scene) or a person – which aspects of the place or person has the writer focused on? Which aspects have been ignored?

Can you sense a character behind the description? In other words, can you tell that the description is by a narrator who is a character in the book, rather than by the author her/himself? How has this been achieved?

What does the description tell you about the person who is doing the describing? Further, what does it tell you about the relationship between the describer and the described? How, precisely, has the author done this?

If the first page consists mostly of dialogue, how are the different voices presented? If not (or rarely) by name, how do the speech patterns and vocabulary that each character uses differentiate her/him from each of the others? [Try cutting out little scraps of paper and covering up the identities of each speaker. Would you still be able to tell, purely from the way they talk, who is saying what?]

Now open the book/story at random and select another paragraph. Ask the same questions. You should now be starting to see how your favourite author achieves many of the effects that you enjoy so much.

Lastly, the one piece of advice that is always and inevitably given to new writers is 'Write about what you know'. Whilst that is very sound advice indeed – for reasons we will come to – all too often it discourages potential writers who feel that their lives have not been as exciting as they might have been; they have never ventured alone into the heart of an unknown city, nor forded swollen rivers, nor hacked their way through impenetrable jungle equipped only with a butter knife, a pair of Wellingtons and a slab of Kendal Mint Cake.

Few of us have, of course, but all of us at one time or another have been children, adults, possibly parents; we have all fallen in love and out of love, made friends and lost touch with them, made enemies and resolved our differences with them (or not!), been happy, sad, desperate, hopeful or resigned. In short, we have all had the experience of reacting to and inter-reacting with a wide range of people in a variety of different circumstances. This experience is unique to each individual, and this is the 'what you know' that will inform all your writing. It is so important that we will be returning to this subject in a later section.

Get the idea

'Where do you get your ideas from?' is one of the most common questions posed to writers at readings or on promotional tours. There are almost as many answers as there are writers, but all too often the process seems mystical. 'I don't really know, they just seem to come,' is a frequent response, but that's not really satisfactory. If we can identify some of the paths these ideas take, we may be able to go out and look for them, rather than just sitting back and waiting for them to turn up. When pushed, most writers will come up with one or more of the following.

Curiosity may have killed the cat, but it is the very essence of a writer's life and, if it doesn't come naturally, should be cultivated. Why did X do that? Why did Y say that? Why are the curtains at number 42 always closed? You are not seeking some sort of objective truth – the 'real' reasons why X, Y and the occupants of number 42 act as they do – but rather the wide range of possibilities that might lead to such behaviour. This, of course, is allied to...

Observation because, quite simply, you can't be curious about what you don't see. Developing a keen sense of observation is absolutely essential if you are to bring to your writing the full richness and complexity of the world around you – the ways in which people react to events and to one another, the expressiveness of a gesture, the colour changes and lengthening shadows as light fades at the end of the day, the ways in which a taste or smell can conjure up memories of other times, other places, other people. You will note from this last example that you, yourself, will also be the subject of your own observations, which brings us to...

Autobiography. Although this can refer to the events of your life – or, to protect the innocent, fictionalised forms of those events – it chiefly refers to the fact that the one person each of us knows most intimately is ourselves. We all have blind spots, but on the whole we are perfectly aware of why we behave as we do, and are therefore the sole authority for our thoughts, words and deeds. Applying this 'insider knowledge' to the observed objects of your curiosity can generate a vast number of ideas. Keep a notebook with you at all times and jot them down!

Exercise

Select one of the pictures on the page opposite, and use your powers of observation to examine it carefully. Don't just look at the focal point of the picture, but also at the detail in the foreground, the background, the periphery.

What do you think is happening in the picture? What are the circumstances that led up to this precise event? What happens next?

Jot down your ideas.

You will find that you now have the rudiments of a story, or at least of an episode in a longer story, but you will probably also find that you have had to discard certain options in order to concentrate on a single set of possibilities.

Put your initial jottings to one side and look at the picture again. How many other stories can you see? Jot each one down on separate pieces of paper. If you are doing this exercise in a group, each member should examine the same picture independently, and jot down her/his initial ideas. When this is done – five minutes should be enough – go round the group and compare notes. How many different stories were uncovered? Several group members may have identified details that other members thought irrelevant, but this can be very useful. Observation is a skill, and learning from others is a very good way of developing it. The more you observe, the greater the number of possible storylines will be revealed

[If you are not part of a group, show the picture to a friend or relative and ask them what they see. You may be surprised how different their story is from yours.]

There are many other ways of generating ideas – reading articles in newspapers or magazines, applying your powers of observation to TV documentaries, even the act of writing itself (where you might suddenly find a story going in directions you hadn't quite expected) – but what underlies all of them is that other important weapon in the writer's armoury, daydreaming: what would have happened if…?

Night-time dreams can be equally important – although often at a later stage, when your unconscious mind continues to work on an idea while you're sleeping – but the great benefit of daydreaming is that it allows you to follow through an idea to see where it leads. In short, it's a form of story writing – or, more accurately, story testing that doesn't require pen and paper …but keep that notebook handy!

Middles

– Developing characters
– Developing plots
– Structures

Notes

Developing characters

At the end of an earlier section (Before we begin...) we looked briefly at the rich variety of personal experience that underlies most creative writing – writing about what you know. It is now time to return to this idea, and raise the related concept of role-playing, which has been borrowed from social psychology.

In the course of our lives we each play a number of different roles, and are often categorised accordingly. We have each been a child, for example, with either parents or guardians, and our behaviour as children was very different from our subsequent behaviour as adults – or so we like to think. We are likely to have also been friends, lovers, spouses, parents and work colleagues, for example, and each of these different 'roles' has a set of behaviours and expectations that defines it. To examine this in more detail, let's try another exercise.

Exercise

Make a list of all the different roles you have played in your life. You will certainly have been a son or a daughter, and you may even be a parent. You may be married, single or divorced, and will either have had a job – perhaps even a succession of them – or you may have spent weeks and months seeking work. The list can be as short and general or as long and detailed as you wish.

Now select one of those roles and examine it in more detail. Each role has a complex network of rules that govern the way we behave in that role, and although nobody writes these rules down, we still manage to absorb them as we go through life. How do we do this? Well, think about the role you've selected – how did you learn to behave in the appropriate way? Did you copy the behaviour of other family members or of friends? Did other people offer you advice or act, quite literally, as role-models? Were the rules very vague and general or narrow and tightly focused? What happened if you 'broke' the rules?

Now focus on an event that illustrates one such learning occasion. This can sometimes be a very uncomfortable thing to do, so pretend that it is happening, now, to someone else. What leads up to the event? Will this person do the same as you once did or something different? How will their actions affect the way their life progresses from this point onwards? How does the episode affect the other people they're involved with?

Congratulations! You now have the makings of a short story, a novel or a play ...and, no matter how disguised, it's based entirely on your own experience.

Spend some more time thinking about roles, behaviours and expectations. You will soon realise that they often give rise to conflict. Children rebel against their parents' expectations, lovers want different things from a relationship, friends' expectations are not met, and so on. By conflict we don't necessarily mean open warfare or hostilities – although it can often escalate into that – but rather the small but often far-reaching disagreements that can be engendered by things not quite matching a person's view of the world. This sort of conflict is central to fiction, because most fiction – be it in the form of short stories, novels or plays – involves the interaction of two or more characters, or the reaction of a central character to her/his social, physical or psychological environment. We all want an easy life, but few of us want to read a book or watch a play in which everyone gets on with everyone else and there are no conflicts to be resolved!

It follows from this that your characters and how you portray them will be crucial to the success of your fiction – you can derive a plot from the interactions of two characters, but you can't derive a character from a plot outline – so let's look at the ways in which this can be achieved.

If your characters are going to seem real to your readers – if their reactions are to be believable – then your reader has to be aware of them as fully rounded personalities, with behavioural traits that also indicate a rich inner 'mental' life. But how can the writer achieve this without presenting each character's point of view as a first person narrative? Time for another exercise.

Exercise

Think about a person that you feel you know quite well (though preferably not a partner, as this can raise all sorts of problems!). First list their good points – what it is that you like about them. Then list their bad points – irritating habits, opinions and attitudes that you don't care for. Now think back to when you first met her or him. Over time, how did you discover the things that you know/feel about them? Try to answer the following questions:

- What was the first thing that struck you about them?
- What did you see as their outstanding physical characteristics?
- How were they dressed, and what did this tell you?
- Did they have any little gestures or ways of speaking that caught your attention?
- Did they maintain eye contact or avoid it?
- Did they seek out physical contact or shrink from it?
- What did they talk about?
- Now that you've got to know them, what do you think motivates* them?
- How does your current level of knowledge differ from your first impressions?
- Finally, what sort of person do you think they really are? Are they straightforward or devious, honest or dishonest, tolerant or intolerant, placid or easily roused, warm-hearted or aloof?

Now for the more difficult part of the task:

Just how, exactly, did you obtain the information that enabled you to answer those last few questions?

If another person told you something that altered your opinion, how accurate was this additional information?

You will almost certainly find that your knowledge of people comes entirely from what they do (their physical actions, including gestures and facial expressions), what they say (their speech actions), and the degree to which these two types of action complement (or fail to complement) one another. A third party report may add to this information, but its accuracy depends on the reliability of the reporter and his/her own set of behaviours, expectations and motives.

As a writer, you should always try to present your characters in this way – through what they say and what they do. This is the essence of what is meant by 'show, don't tell'. A character's factual history might not be important to the story, but the sort of person they are most certainly is.

*What motivates a person – and therefore what drives your characters – will be determined by their own personal histories. There are many ways of characterising motivators – you may be able to think of many more yourself – but consider the following as a starting point:

- Love, ranging from physical to spiritual
- Money and possessions
- Power, or control over others
- Survival, which can range from concerns over health through to a struggle against enemies
- Revenge, which can be full-blooded, or as simple as getting your own back on someone
- Approval of others, ranging from the wish to be liked, right through to striving for fame
- Personal integrity and notions of self-worth – a sort of psychological survival

Developing plots

In the previous section we suggested that, although you can derive a plot from the interactions of two characters, you can't really derive a character from a bare plot outline. Let's examine that in a little more detail.

Two characters, A and B, are rivals for X (X can either be a third character, an object, or some other sort of goal). How the story subsequently unfolds – the plot, if you like – depends not on the mere fact of their rivalry, but on the different stratagems that A and B employ in order to attain the prize, the ways in which they try to thwart their rival, and the lengths they will go to in order to do so. In short, the storyline depends entirely on what A and B are like as people. (It's worth pointing out that the **type** of story depends on you, the author. The above plot could either be an adventure story, a love story, or the sort of story in which the psychological development of one or both characters becomes more important than the goal.)

Although character development is central to plot development, many writers like to start with a situation or event and then create characters who will respond to it in a certain way. This is a perfectly legitimate way of working, although you have to be careful to avoid creating stereotypes rather than full rounded characters, and there's always a danger that your characters might decide to take the plot in directions you hadn't considered!

You may have a number of plots in mind already perhaps generated by the first exercise in the previous section – but in case you're stuck for inspiration you could try the following exercise and produce your own multi-plot generator.

Exercise

- Down the left hand side of a sheet of A4 paper list the numbers 0 to 9.
- Across the top of the page write four column headings – Character, Location, Object and Motive.
- Ask a friend to give you a list of ten types of people or ten occupations (for example sailor, beach photographer, housewife). Under the Character column, write them down against the numbers 0 to 9 (the order is irrelevant).
- Ask a different friend for ten locations. These can be specific (Notre Dame Cathedral in Paris, for example) or very general (a hairdressing salon, a refugee camp). List these under the Location column against the numbers 0 to 9.
- Now ask a third friend to name ten different things – such as a teddy bear, a signed photograph, a football etc. List these under Object.
- Complete the fourth column yourself, using the motivators identified in the previous section. There were only seven and you need ten, so either duplicate some of them, intersperse them with three labelled 'Unknown', or come up with some new ones of your own.
- When the table is complete, ask several people to provide you with a series of four-digit numbers, anything from 0000 to 9999.

Each four-digit number will now provide you with the bare bones of a plot. The number 4057, for example, will give you Character 4 in Location 0 with Object 5, and the plot will be driven by Motive 7.

Now try to draft a story using these four elements – there are literally thousands to choose from. The plot can be as wild and wacky as you want it to be – the main aim is to get you writing, and to stimulate your imagination – but, who knows, you may turn up something that really gets your creative juices flowing.

(You will find an example of such a plot generator in the Resource section of this book. The format is slightly different, but the principle is just the same.)

Structures

At the heart of all stories lies a sequence of linked chronological events, although the story itself may not depict all the events or necessarily depict them in chronological order. Short stories, in particular, often start at or just before a key event, and the backstory (what happened before the 'real' story started, including the history of each character) only emerges if – and when – it is essential to an understanding of the story.

As we have already seen, a story consists of one or more central characters in a situation (often involving other characters) which produces some form of conflict (most often as the result of the interaction between the characters) that requires a resolution. There are said to be only a finite number of plots – the exact number has been recorded as 5, 7 or 20, depending on the source (although 7 seems to be the most popular) – but probably a more useful way of categorising stories is to look at the deep structures that underlie them, structures that most readers are psychologically predisposed to expect. They are:

The Search...

in which the main character – the traditional hero or heroine suits this particular structural form well – is given a task (the situation), achievement of which is obstructed by a number of obstacles to be overcome (the conflict) before the goal is reached (resolution). At its simplest level, this structure underlies such stories as Jason and the Golden Fleece, and Lord of the Rings – not to mention the vast majority of 'action' movies – but it is by no means limited to physical situations and obstacles. A number of stories and novels centre on the main character's quest for self realisation and the obstacles largely take the form of other people's contradictory expectations. In diagrammatic terms it's like a rising graph with a series of ever-higher peaks, culminating in the highest peak, the final showdown.

Closing the Circle...

in which the main character finds her/his life (the situation) is threatened by an intruder (the conflict) that must be battled until the status quo is either reinstated or refashioned (the resolution).

Such a structure underlies Beowulf, for example, not to mention most ghost stories and thousands of westerns (think of High Noon) but, again, neither the threat nor the situation need be so physical. In diagrammatic form, this is like a circle that has been broken and needs to be made whole again.

Squaring the Circle...

in which the main character finds her/his life (the situation) affected in a more or less welcome way by an outsider (the conflict), the resolution of the story depending on the degree to which the protagonists successfully resolve their differences. This is the traditional romance, if you like, and is a reverse form of Closing the Circle. Diagrammatically, it is the gradual process by which a square and a circle alter their shapes in order to resemble one another.

If you can analyse your own story in these simple structural terms, you should be able to tell if you have tried to incorporate elements of more than one structure at the same time, thereby failing to meet audience expectations at a very basic level. There is nothing wrong with testing your audience's expectations, but you should always be aware that you are testing them, why you are testing them and, hopefully, your audience should ultimately be aware of this too. It is entirely feasible to incorporate more than one structure, particularly in a novel, but the main plot should adhere to one of the above structures (a Search, for example) whilst the sub-plots could depend upon a different structure (such as Squaring the Circle). This sort of structural integration underlies adventure stories that have romantic sub-plots, but you should beware of creating a central plot that combines multiple structures simultaneously. The other advantage of analysing your story like this, is that it may give you an insight into the best starting point, which should be just before the first conflict point. If you start too early you risk boring your audience, too late and you risk having to catch up on too much backstory.

That just about takes us to the end of this section, and to the most demanding exercise yet. You will probably still have a lot of questions – we hope to answer most of them in the next section – but now it's time to get down to some real writing.

Exercise

Taking, as your starting point, one of the stories that suggested itself during earlier exercises, or even the original idea that brought you to this book in the first place, write at least the first few paragraphs. You may not yet know if it will turn into a short story or a novel, but the important thing is to start writing.

Don't worry if you feel a bit lost at this stage – that's deliberate. Writing is a skill that you learn more about by making mistakes than by getting it right – whatever that means – and the next section will provide you with a number of techniques that will enable you to analyse this first draft and make vast improvements. What is essential is that you at least overcome the fear of writing that difficult first sentence, and then see where it leads you.

If you are totally unsure as to where to start, try analysing your story in terms of the structures we have just discussed. Identify the first conflict point, and start there. Rather than set the scene with a description, try getting straight into the action. How about starting with a line of dialogue and seeing where it leads you?

Again, the important thing is that you start to write. There is no time limit, but try to complete a full story – or the first chapter of a longer story – if you can. That said, don't worry if you get no further than the first few paragraphs. Only you will ever see this early draft, so there is nothing to fear. Get writing!

Endings

- Editing and rewriting
- Marketing your work

Notes

Editing and rewriting

Editing

The first draft of any piece of writing is a bit like the rough shape that a sculptor first blocks out of the marble. Thereafter, it's a process of chipping away to reveal the final statue. As far as writing is concerned, your reader will focus on any redundant material, causing them to falter when they should read seamlessly on. Similarly, cut out too much and your reader will, quite literally, lose the plot and quickly lose interest. The editing stage, in other words, is where the hard work – and the true craft of writing – really begins.

Of course there are writers who are capable of producing perfectly weighted prose automatically, with little need for second thoughts, but that is certainly not universally true nor even very common. The vast majority spend weeks, months, even years honing their work to the point where the reader's understanding of the text matches exactly the writer's intentions. This might involve, at a macro level, the complete rewriting of the piece – involving quite complex changes to plot or character – but at a micro level it's all about language and punctuation, rhythm and pace, consistency and balance. There are no hard-and-fast rules about this – the ultimate criterion is whether a piece works or not – but the following suggestions may help. (From now on the exercises are almost entirely based on your own work.)

Openings and closings

Before we get down to the fine detail, let's look at opening sentences. The aim of a first sentence is to capture the reader's interest and imagination. Ideally, it should combine an element of scene-setting with an element of anticipation. Take the following quotation, for example, which is the opening sentence of Ernest Hemingway's story 'The Short Happy Life of Francis Macomber':

> *"It was now lunch time and they were all sitting under the double green fly of the dining tent pretending that nothing had happened."*

In two dozen words we are aware that the story takes place on a camping expedition – a fairly up-market one at that, given the separate dining tent – that it involves more than one character, and that something fairly dramatic has happened. The event is so dramatic, in fact, that no one can talk about it, but we don't yet know if this is because of the immensity of the event or because of the psychological make-up of the characters. How could any reader not want to discover more?

This is an ideal, of course, and you shouldn't expect to come up with such an opening sentence at your first attempt. In fact it would be fair to say that few writers manage to produce an opening of such power and economy on a regular basis – but that shouldn't prevent you from trying! What you may find, however, is that there is a striking sentence near the start of your story, just that it isn't the first sentence.

Exercise

Cover up the opening paragraph of your story, and read on as if the second paragraph were where the story began. How much sense, if any, has been lost? If a key piece of information is missing, can it be equally well presented later in the piece? If nothing has been lost, try covering up the second paragraph and imagine that the story starts with the third paragraph.

You will probably find – as a lot of writers do – that the opening of your first draft has been more of a warming up exercise, a way of breaking yourself in gently to the often daunting task of filling that first blank page. Oddly enough, 'false' openings like this can persist through any number of drafts, and it's only when you actively seek to eliminate them and find that nothing has been lost that you understand what has been happening.

If you reached the end of your story – or when you finally do get there – try covering up the final paragraph. Again, how much, if anything, has been lost? As with beginnings, so with endings, unnecessary material often persisting through version after version. It reflects the fact that you are unwilling to let go of something to which you have become deeply attached – the very act of writing the story itself, perhaps – but you have to be ruthless. Even the most exquisitely written sentence you have ever produced must be sacrificed if it has no place in the story.

Over the years you will probably develop an instinct about this – knowing exactly where to start and when to finish – but you should always be aware of the possibility of 'writing your way in', even if you are a published writer.

Language

English is a remarkably complex language, its subtleties stemming from the fact that it is rooted in a wide variety of languages including Latin, Greek, French, German and Norse. It is therefore a very powerful language for conveying nuances of thought, and you should never be afraid of using dictionaries and a thesaurus to ensure that you select precisely the right word for your purpose.

Practical examples are always the best, and examples that are unique to your own work are always going to be more meaningful, so return to your story and try the following.

Exercise

1. Firstly, underline each adverb and the verb that it qualifies. [Adverbs are words like 'quickly' or 'silently' that qualify – i.e. give further meaning to – verbs]. Where adverbs occur in dialogue you can leave them in – characters won't be following the same rules that you are! – but every adverb in the narrative should be justifiable. Verbs are extremely powerful – they drive your work along – and they don't need much help, so open your thesaurus and find the precise verb for the job. If one character is following another character quickly, for example, you could have pursue, chase or hound instead of follow quickly, and your sentence will be all the stronger for it. Of course, if you can't find a verb that gives you the exact shade of meaning, then consider retaining the adverb, but your goal should always be to get the most precise meaning in the fewest possible words. This will give your work freshness and vividness.
2. In the same way, underline each adjective. [Adjectives are words that qualify – i.e. describe – a noun]. Eliminating adjectives is perhaps not quite as important as eliminating adverbs, but too many – particularly lists of adjectives – will soon stifle your reader's imagination. To understand the importance of imagination to reading, consider how many people say that such-and-such an actor wasn't how they imagined the character in the book. If you go back to the book, you will often find that the character wasn't described at all! Some adjectives are essential, of course – colours, for example – but most can be omitted without affecting the work in the slightest. Try it and see – you can always put them back.
3. Now take a look at the length of your sentences. Are they long and complex, or short and pithy? If the length varies throughout the piece, are they randomly varied or does there seem to be some sort of correlation between sentence length and content? In general, you will find that long sentences slow the action down, while short sentences speed it up, and many writers do this unconsciously to control the pace of a narrative. You should normally aim for an equal balance of long and short sentences, but knowing about the phenomenon allows you to use it to your own advantage, altering the balance to suit the pace of your work.

Dialogue

Rather than have page after solid page of unbroken narrative or description – which is hard on the eye, and can be daunting for the reader – it is best to intersperse patches of narrative with dialogue, allowing your characters to speak for themselves rather than have you reporting what they say to each other or themselves.

Whether writing a novel or a short story, dialogue should always serve some purpose – it should either advance the plot or develop a character, preferably both at the same time. Dialogue should never simply be small talk or conversation for its own sake ...or simply because you happen to like the line.

No exercise this time, just a few suggestions that may help. Read them carefully, then go back to your story to see how you can put them into practice.

- Always try to write dialogue that doesn't require you to tell the reader – through narrative – how it is to be said. For example, have a character use words that make her/his anger clear rather that having to add 'she/he snapped'.
- Be aware that dialogue doesn't have to follow the grammatical and syntactical rules of English that you would use in the narrative, but at the same time avoid the 'ums' and 'ers' that practically everyone uses in daily speech (unless you want to make a specific point about a character's indecision).
- Dialogue is often a fencing match – one speaker doesn't always let the other speaker have her/his full say. Used carefully, this sort of broken interchange can help speed up the action and/or add to character development.
- 'She/he said' is merely a pointer as to who is speaking, nothing else. Even in a full page of dialogue, unbroken by narrative, you should only need to use such pointers at every third or fourth exchange, or where it might be unclear which of the characters is speaking at that point.
- Just as full pages of narrative or description can put a reader off, so can full pages of dialogue. People do not stop what they're doing in order to speak, and speech is often a response to action, not just to another speech, so try to vary it.

- Elegant variations of 'she/he said' – 'he exclaimed', 'she riposted', 'she declaimed', 'he retorted' etc – are no longer fashionable, and are nowadays seen as amateurish. They draw attention to themselves, not to what is being said, and often contain information that already exists (or should exist!) in the dialogue itself. Strangely enough, 'she/he said', since it's nothing more than an indicator of who is speaking, is normally invisible to the reader.
- Dialect and slang should be used sparingly, just to give a flavour of how a character speaks. Slang dates quickly and dialect doesn't travel far – your writing should be understandable twenty years from now and several hundred miles away.

Rewriting

If you have been through all the above processes and you still feel that something is not quite right with your story, consider the following.

Is the central character the focal point of the piece? Perhaps the story really belongs to another character – so why not try rewriting it from his/her point of view? Perhaps a younger character might add more risk, or an older one more gravitas.

Have you based your work too closely on your own life/experiences? Perhaps you need to get more distance, so why not change the gender of the main character? This may enable you to be more objective.

Is the voice right? The story may feel completely different if it's written in the first person ('I'), the third person ('he/she') or, on occasion, the second person ('you'). Try rewriting it in each voice in turn, to see which works best. Perhaps some parts work best in one voice, other parts in another. Could it be possible that the story contains two different voices, or is it because there's something wrong with the way you're presenting one of the characters?

Are time and place right for the story that you want to tell? Perhaps you've set the action in the present day, when the behaviour of the characters might be more appropriate to the 1960s, or in the country, when it should really be an urban story. Try rewriting it in a different context.

Is there too much 'backstory' [the history of the characters prior to the action of the story itself]? You want your readers to look forwards, not backwards, and you're not going to achieve this if you are constantly feeding them bits of historical information. If this history is essential to the plot, then why not start the story earlier? If it's not essential, then why are you telling us? [The 'backstory' of all your characters is something that you need to know about – it helps you bring your characters to life – but only certain parts of their histories will be relevant to the present action.]

Finally

...read your story aloud! If you are a member of a writers' group then you will have plenty of opportunity for this, but you should get into the habit of doing so even when you are on your own. There are two reasons for this: firstly, you will get a much clearer idea of the rhythm of your sentences, the natural rise and fall that is as essential to the reader's eye as it is to the listener's ear; secondly, you will find yourself stumbling over clumsy phrases and ambiguous sentences – exactly the sort of thing that will catch your readers' eye and distract them. It may not be obvious, but even silent reading relies on the 'inner' ear, and anything that prevents your readers from concentrating on the story is to be avoided at all costs.

Notes

Marketing your work

Getting published

Submitting your work for publication can be a fraught process, but it's one that you have to go through, again and again, if your work is not to gather dust. If you never send your work out then the one thing that can be guaranteed is that it will never be published. But who do you send it to?

The first thing to note is that you will usually stand a better chance of placing your work with a publisher if you can avail yourself of the services of a literary agent. You will find lists of such agents in **The Writers' Handbook** [MacMillan] or **The Writers' and Artists' Yearbook** [A&C Black], both published annually, but the catch is that agents are as hard to attract as publishers! Like publishers, they exist to make money – a percentage of the author's literary income – and so are unlikely to take on a writer whose work they aren't convinced that they can sell. For budding novelists who don't have an agent, the only advice is to do some research.

It should be obvious, but you will not sell a romance to a house that only publishes science fiction, or a piece of literary fiction to one that publishes only westerns. Research your market carefully, and at least you will end up on the right slush pile. The slush pile refers to all the unsolicited manuscripts that a publisher receives. They lie around until someone – usually a new employee – is given the job of wading through them and, usually, returning them whence they came. (Occasionally you can be lucky – the winner of the 2003 Man Booker Prize, DBC Pierre's **Vernon God Little** allegedly came from such a pile.) You will stand a better chance if the publisher has actually asked to see your work – if you have sent in advance a specimen chapter or two plus a synopsis, rather than a whole book – but this is very unlikely to happen unless you have an agent to promote you. Back to square one.

An awful lot depends on the sort of work you write. In the case of the short story writer (or the poet), few mainstream publishers accept work from untried writers. Fortunately, however, a huge network of small presses exists purely to promote such work, although few of them publish novels.

There are more than 500 small press magazines in the UK, most of them publishing poetry but some reserving space for fiction writers. Both **The Writer's Handbook** and the **Writers' and Artists' Yearbook** list a large proportion of the national small presses – plus some abroad – and try to give an indication of the sort of work they prefer. Alternatively, if you're only interested in small presses, try the relatively newer **The Magazine Writer's Handbook** [Forward Publishing]. You'll get a far better idea of a magazine's suitability, however, if you select a handful of the most promising candidates and send off for a specimen copy (if you tell them why you want it – to see if what you write could be suitable for them – they may even send you a back issue at a reduced rate). Look on it as an investment, not an expense. Some larger bookshops also carry directories of writers' markets in the USA. The market is much bigger than in the UK, but not necessarily easier to get into.

These days, many magazines promote themselves via the web, so if you have access to the Internet you could do worse than to type 'short story magazines' into a search engine such as Google and browse through the millions of resultant links. Some magazines even publish directly online rather than producing copies in print format but, in general, the same principle applies to all – check your market carefully before submitting.

The financial gains you stand to make from small press publication are infinitesimal, of course. Some magazines do pay for work that appears – say £5 per poem, or £15-£20 per story – but the vast majority are run on a shoestring by a single editor who simply can't afford to pay contributors (most are lucky to be able to pay the print bill!). You will, however, receive a complimentary copy of the issue that your work appears in.

That said, the small presses are often an integral part of a writer's apprenticeship, because you are compelled to satisfy the requirements of a specific editor who knows what his/her readers want. Once a particular magazine has accepted a piece from you, the chances of them doing so again are improved, but the main benefit is that you will have the confidence to send work to more magazines, with a covering letter listing the other magazine(s) in which your work has appeared. This will not make a difference to the final decision of a good editor – he/she will still only accept what they actually like – but it will mean that your work is read more attentively, not just skimmed.

Once your work has appeared in a number of different magazines, it may be time to approach a small press that publishes collections, not just magazines, although you should bear in mind that very few mainstream publishers produce collections of short stories, so you may have to switch to writing novels!

Whether you are sending work to a publisher, an agent or the editor of a small press magazine, one rule is sacrosanct: you must always accompany your work with a stamped self-addressed envelope for the reply, making sure that the envelope is big enough to take the manuscript if you want it back. Small press magazines, for example, receive hundreds of submissions each year, and they simply can't afford to subsidise such costs, but even mainstream publishers and agents are more likely to reply if you send an SAE.

Vanity publishing v self-publishing

If you look through any magazine aimed at writers – and there are a number on the market – you will find a number of companies offering to publish your novel, autobiography or poetry or story collection. They will offer editorial assistance, arrange for the final work to be printed and bound, and undertake promotion and distribution – at a price. This industry is known as vanity publishing, and it exists to satisfy the writer's burning, and very understandable, desire to see her/his work in print.

To a degree, the majority of such companies do exactly what they promise, but the process will set you back several thousand pounds and simply being in print is no guarantee that your work will sell or be read. This is true of all published work, of course, but at least mainstream publishers will back their belief in you by publishing and promoting it at their own expense – and may even give you a modest advance against future sales. Vanity publishers, on the other hand, expect you to take all the financial risk. You should also be wary of competitions that cost nothing to enter, but that offer winners publication in a 'sumptuously bound' anthology ...that can be bought at a special price. Needless to say, everyone's a winner!

If you are so desperate to see your work in print that cost is irrelevant, then by all means go ahead, but if you really want your work to be appreciated for itself, then you will just have to persevere with mainstream publishers and hope that one of them will finally see the talent that you know you possess. If your work is good enough, then it will sell. Any offer to publish your work at a price should be avoided.

Self-publishing, although it bears some superficial similarities, is not quite the same. For one thing it means a lot of hard work on your part, but it's undeniably cheaper than vanity publishing and you are entirely in control of your own destiny. At the most basic level, all you need is a manuscript and the services of a good local printer, most of whom will help with cover design and book layout, though it will be cheaper if you are able to do the basic typesetting yourself. The printer will give you a quote covering the cost of design, setting, layout, printing, binding and delivery.

What you then do with the finished product is up to you, but be very cautious about the number of copies you ask for. The cost per copy is much cheaper the more you get printed, but you will have to be realistic. Once every member of your family and all your friends have one, what is the size of your remaining audience? Local newspapers and local radio stations are always on the lookout for good human interest stories, so they may provide you with one channel for publicity, but you really need to get your book into bookshops if it's to stand a chance in what is a very crowded market.

To do this, you will have to become a publisher yourself. Your book will need an ISBN (International Standard Book Number), a bar code (so that the price can be processed through electronic till systems) and, preferably, a printed spine (booksellers simply don't have the space to display books face-on). Inevitably, this all adds to the cost, but – who knows? – you may even decide to go on and publish others in the same position as yourself. For more information on becoming a publisher, contact Nielsen BookData, the UK ISBN Agency, on http://www.nbdrs.com/isbn_agency.htm

Competitions

One final way of testing your talent is by entering one of the many short story (and poetry) competitions, and the best way of finding out about these is by entering Short Story (or Poetry) Competitions into an Internet search engine such as Google. Most offer prize money – which is why you will be required to send a modest fee with your entry – but some may offer publication as well. Needless to say, they attract hundreds of entries and can be something of a lottery, but then so is sending your work to a publisher, agent or editor.

In the end you just have to persevere. As we said at the start of this book, financial gain should be the last reason for starting to write!

Resource section

- The inspiration file
- The daily task
- Character questionnaire
- Sample plot generator
- Afterword

Notes

The inspiration file

Every creative writing tutor in the world will tell you this, but it's still worth repeating: **keep a notebook and pen to hand at all times**. You never know when inspiration is going to strike and, like dreams, good ideas quickly fade if not written down immediately. But what, exactly, are you going to jot down? Ideas for new work, obviously, but try these as well:

- Dreams and daydreams – when your mind isn't focussed on anything in particular, it often throws up connections that wouldn't normally be made.
- Snippets of conversation that you hear around you – at home, in the pub, on the bus, in the supermarket check-out queue. Don't just concentrate on **what** people say but also on **how** they say it. The varieties and nuances of speech are essential to a writer.
- Descriptions of people (including gestures and mannerisms) or locations, either from real life or from TV. Next time you're on holiday, try keeping a detailed daily diary instead of taking photographs.
- From books, write down quotations and references that excite your interest – either for their content or for their style.
- Newspaper/magazine articles that catch your eye. [Thomas Hardy used to copy out news items from his local paper. Some of the scenes in **Tess of the D'Urbervilles**, for example, have their real-life counterparts in 19th Century Dorset.]
- Photographs, whether your own, or from newspapers and magazines (you will have realised by now that you're going to need more than just a notebook).

The very fact that you've noticed these things makes them important, even if the reason for their importance is not immediately apparent. Your unconscious mind has flagged them as things worth noting, and you would be well advised to leave it to work on the connections. It can take days, weeks, months or even years, but one day you will know why that particular item caught your eye.

So, what are you going to do with all this material? Different writers have different storage and retrieval methods – such as indexed card files or even shoeboxes – but why not invest in a few loose-leaf folders and a pack of A4 plastic pockets? You can keep separate folders for different projects – plus a general folder, for things that don't yet fit anywhere – and can file, sort and resort the material to your heart's content.

The daily task

Setting aside some part of each day in which to write is not easy for most people – the conflicting demands of job, family and social life tend to fill our waking hours with nothing to spare. The habit of writing each day is a good one to cultivate, however, so it's well worth making the effort.

- Draw a grid with separate squares for each waking hour of each day. For at least a week, keep an hourly record of how you spend your time – job, meals, shopping, visiting friends or relatives, watching TV etc. If there are gaps, why not use those times to write? If there are no gaps, take a hard look at how you fill your time. Do you watch TV simply out of habit? Why not replace it with the habit of writing? Still stumped? Try getting up an hour earlier!
- Once you have identified your time slots, think about your writing environment. Somewhere quiet helps, but the main thing is lack of distraction. At a desk near a window through which you can gaze may not be a good idea, nor is a table in the room where the family is watching TV. Bedrooms and kitchens are better, and the writer who has a private study or a habitable garden shed should consider her/himself truly blessed.
- Don't get hung up about the writing method. The important thing is to get your ideas down on the page, and it's absolutely irrelevant whether you do so via pen, pencil, typewriter, PC, scrap of paper, reporter's notebook, ruled A4 pad, hand-made paper or vellum.
- Beware of the 'sharpening pencils' syndrome – the often unconscious tendency to find a hundred little tasks to do (feeding the cat, alphabetically sorting your CDs) the moment you're supposed to start writing. It may seem like an irritant but it's actually fear – the fear of writing. Learn to recognise it for what it is.

- Always fill your writing time with writing, even if you feel you have nothing to say. Write down anything – what you've done that day, a rant against the iniquities of a world that doesn't give you enough time for writing, a moan about your 'writer's block' – anything that will get you into the habit of putting your thoughts down on paper. Look on it as a warming up exercise.
- Never stop your day's writing at a point where you've run out of ideas – when you start again the next day, you are likely to be still in that negative frame of mind. It's far better to stop halfway through a paragraph – even halfway through a sentence – and just jot down a few notes to remind yourself of where you are going. That way, you'll be all the more keen to start again and won't have that dreadful 'blank page, blank mind' feeling.
- Alternatively, when you run out of ideas, stop writing and try not to fret about it. Better still, sleep on it. Chances are good that your unconscious mind will continue to work on the problem and provide you with a solution the following day. If you are not going to start writing first thing next morning, then be particularly careful to carry a notebook wherever you go! (These two pieces of advice are not as contradictory as they may seem. Not all writers work the same way and each day is different – use the strategy which suits you best.)
- Quality is far better than quantity, so don't be discouraged if you find you're only writing about 500 words a day. That works out at around 180,000 words a year – enough for two average-sized novels or one blockbuster!

Character questionnaire

Although the history of each of your characters is unlikely to appear in your work, it is important that you, the writer, have the fullest possible picture of their lives and influences. This is arguably more important in the novel – which usually has more characters to deal with – but even the short story writer should be aware of each 'backstory'. To give you an idea of what you should be looking for, here's the sort of questionnaire you should complete for each of your characters. It is by no means exhaustive, so try to come up with a few categories of your own.

If you are planning to write a novel, it may be a good idea to keep a 'fact file' like this for each of your characters on index cards. This would include background information, but could be regularly updated with essential new information as the story progresses.

Name: ....

Age: ....

Education: ....

Physical appearance: ....

Mannerisms: ....

Dress: ....

Residence: ....

Occupation: ....

Family: ....

Friends: ....

Pets: ....

Pastimes: ....

Politics: ....

Religion: ....

Strengths: ....

Weaknesses: ....

Obsessions: ....

Ambitions: ....

Likes/dislikes: ....

Favourite brands: ....

Favourite books, movies etc: ....

Desires: ....

Fears: ....

Major turning points in life: ....

Sample plot generator

	Person #1	Person #2	Location	Object
0	rock star	door-to-door salesperson	refugee camp	skull
1	yourself	police officer	revolving door	copy of the Koran
2	priest	actor	deserted beach	complete works of Shakespeare
3	poet	stripper	airport departure lounge	wristwatch
4	horticulturalist	tailor	hotel bedroom	signed photograph
5	homemaker	journalist	ruined city	Gucci handbag
6	lecturer	stand-up comedian	theme park	year old newspaper
7	archaeologist	asylum seeker	country cottage	length of rope
8	dog walker	refuse collector	the summit of a hill	magnum of champagne
9	accident victim	motorbike courier	artist's studio	handgun

Afterword

We hope that this book has given you a taste for writing, and a number of ideas and techniques to get you started. If you would like to take your interest further, and find that this particular way of studying is to your taste, the Open University now offers a number of formal Creative Writing courses. They can be studied independently, purely out of interest, but all carry credit points that be counted towards a qualification at university level.

The following three courses each run for 12 weeks, have a number of different starting points throughout the year, and provide you with all the materials you will need plus a personal tutor. They are delivered electronically, with on-line group tutorials and internet-based resources, so you will need to have access to a PC with internet connections. All three are Level 1 courses, which means that the standard of teaching and learning is the same as you might expect in the first year of a conventional university degree, and each is worth 10 credit points.

A174 Start Writing Fiction

A175 Start Writing Poetry

A176 Start Writing Plays

Based on the success of these short courses, the Open University has devised a much more intensive Level 2 course in Creative Writing worth 60 credit points:

A215 Creative Writing

A215 is intended to provide a complete Creative Writing course from ways to jump-start your writing right through to ways to present your work to agents and publishers: It has five parts.

1. The Creative Process gives practice in ways to free up your writing and gather ideas, chiefly by keeping a writer's notebook. It also explores how best to use and combine memory, experience and research.

2. Writing Fiction gives practice in the main narrative strategies, including character, setting, point of view, showing and telling, structure, and genre.
3. Writing Poetry gives practice in the main elements of the craft, exploring the drafting process, line, voice, imagery, rhyme, form, and theme.
4. Life Writing explores the possible motivations and purposes behind various forms of biography and autobiography and gives practice in a wide range of approaches, building on what you have learned about writing both prose and poetry in earlier parts of the course.
5. Going Public gives you a practical grounding in editing your work to a professional standard and advises you on identifying suitable markets and taking your first steps towards possible publication.

(Potential students who have not studied at university level before would be strongly advised to study one of the Level 1 courses before progressing to A215).

Full details and costs of all the above courses – plus a host of others that may be of particular interest to writers, including courses on literature, history, psychology and philosophy – can be found at our website: www.open.ac.uk or by calling our Student Registration and Enquiry service on 0845 300 60 90.

If this method of studying is not to your taste, or you don't have access to the internet, you may find that there are a number of evening classes in your area, run by local colleges or by the Workers Educational Association (WEA). For details of these you should contact your local library.

Finally, a brief word about writers' groups. Joining a writers' group can be the best way for new writers to get feedback on their work, by reading it aloud and gauging the audience's response. The process is mutual and you will be expected to give constructive criticism on the work of others, not only identifying what doesn't and does work for you but also saying why.

Good luck!

Shortcuts

Notes